MW00816869

CONTEMPO

2ND EDITION

Characters and artwork © Disney Enterprises, Inc./Pixar

ISBN 978-0-634-04515-8

7777 W. BLUEMOUND RD. P.O. BOX 13819 MILWAUKEE, WI 53213

Visit Hal Leonard Online at
www.halleonard.com

ALMOST THERE

from THE PRINCESS AND THE FROG

Music and Lyrics by
RANDY NEWMAN

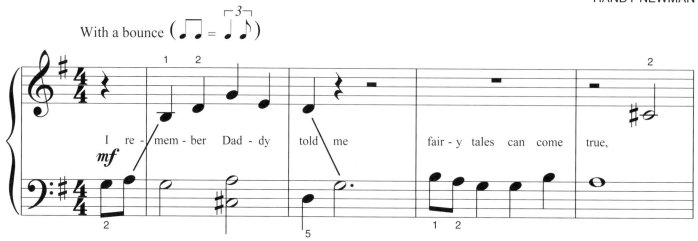

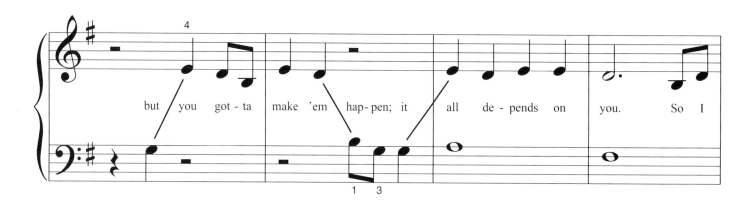

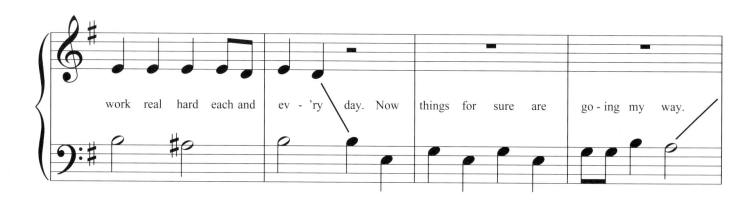

al - most there, I'm al - most there.

Peo - ple gon - na come here from ev - 'ry - where and I'm al - most there, I'm

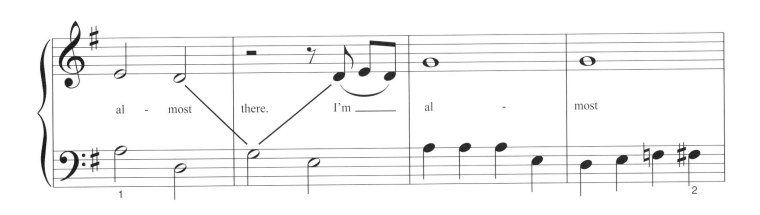

al - most there. I'm ___ al - most

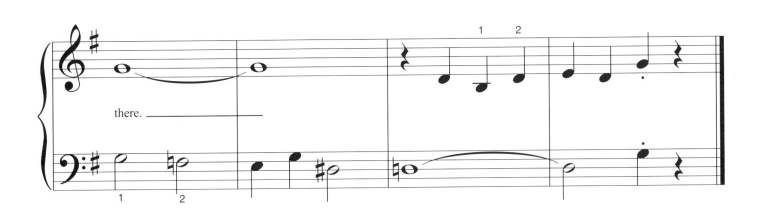

there. ___

FOR THE FIRST TIME IN FOREVER

from FROZEN

Music and Lyrics by KRISTEN ANDERSON-LOPEZ
and ROBERT LOPEZ

With excitement

The win-dow is o - pen! So's that door! I did - n't know they did that an - y - more. Who

knew we owned eight thou-sand sal - ad plates? For years I roamed these emp - ty halls.

Why have a ball - room with no balls? Fi - nal - ly, they're o - p'ning up the

gates! There'll be ac - tual real live peo - ple;

it'll be to - tal - ly strange. But, wow! Am I so read - y for this

change! _____ 'Cause for the first time in for - ev - er, there'll be

mu - sic, there'll be light. ____ For the

first time in for - ev - er, I'll be danc - ing through the

night. Don't know if I'm e - lat - ed or gas - sy, but I'm

some - where in that zone. 'Cause for the first time in for -

ev - er, I won't be a - lone.

HE'S A PIRATE

from PIRATES OF THE CARIBBEAN: THE CURSE OF THE BLACK PEARL

Music by HANS ZIMMER,
KLAUS BADELT and GEOFFREY ZANELLI

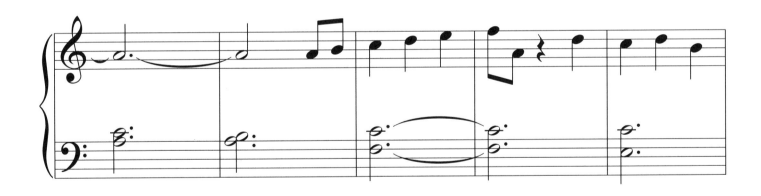

I SEE THE LIGHT
from TANGLED

Music by ALAN MENKEN
Lyrics by GLENN SLATER

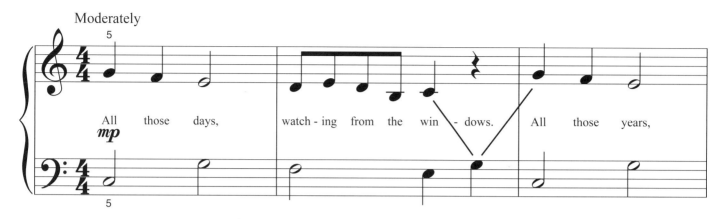

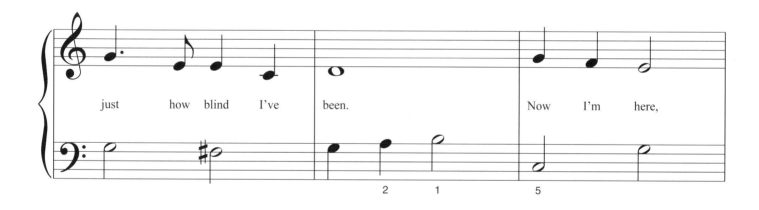

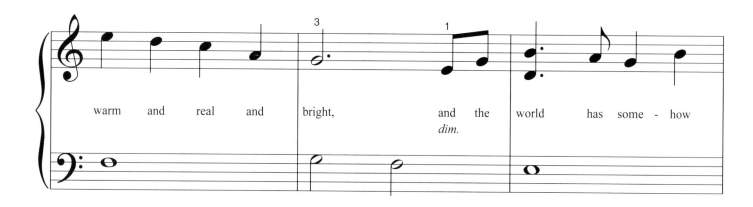

warm and real and bright, and the world has some-how
dim.

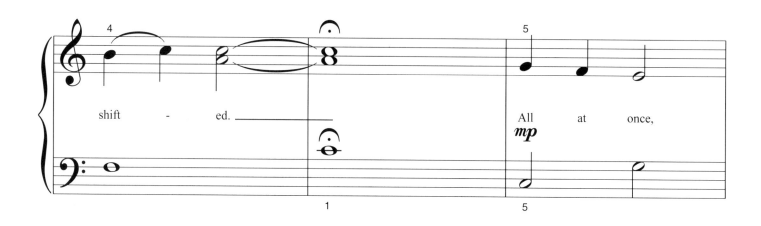

shift - ed. _____ All at once,
mp

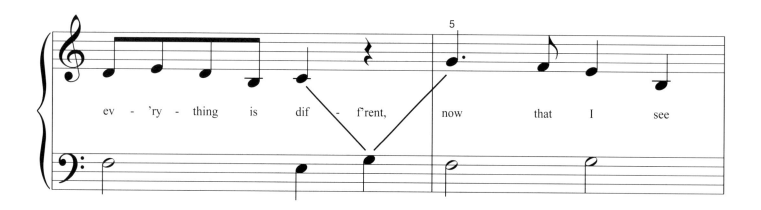

ev - 'ry - thing is dif - f'rent, now that I see

you. Now that I see you.

LAVA
from LAVA

Music and Lyrics by
JAMES FORD MURPHY

A long, long time a - go, there was a vol - ca - no
But lit - tle did he know, that liv - ing in the sea be - low,
(See additional lyrics)

liv - ing all a - lone in the mid - dle of the sea.
an - oth - er vol - ca - no was list - 'ning to his song.

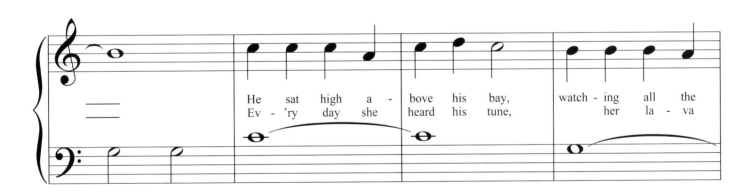

He sat high a - bove his bay, watch - ing all the
Ev - 'ry day she heard his tune, her la - va

cou - ples play be - cause and wish - ing that he had some - one,
grew and grew, she be - lieved his song was meant for

too. _____ _____ And from his la - va came this song of hope
her. _____ _____ Now she was so read - y to meet him a -

that he sang out loud ev - 'ry day for years and years. _____
bove the sea as he sang his song of hope for the last time. _____

_____ "I have a dream I hope will come true, that

you're here with me and I'm here with you. I wish that the

earth, sea and the sky up a - bove - a will send me some - one to

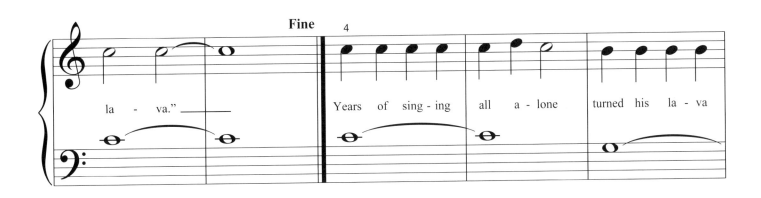

la - va." Years of sing - ing all a - lone turned his la - va

in - to stone, un - til he was on the brink of ex - tinc - tion.

Additional Lyrics

Rising from the sea below stood a lovely volcano,
Looking all around, but she could not see him.
He tried to sing to let her know that she was not there alone,
But with no lava his song was all gone.

He filled the sea with his tears, and watched his dreams disappear
As she remembered what his song meant to her.

I have a dream I hope will come true,
That you're here with me, and I'm here with you.
I wish that the earth, sea, and the sky up above-a
Will send me someone to lava.

Oh, they were so happy to fin'lly meet above the sea.
All together now their lava grew and grew.
No longer are they all alone, with aloha as their new home,
And when you visit them this is what they sing.

I have a dream I hope will come true,
That you'll grow old with me, and I'll grow old with you.
We thank you earth, sea, and the sky we thank too,
I lava you. I lava you. I lava you.

LET IT GO
from FROZEN

Music and Lyrics by KRISTEN ANDERSON-LOPEZ
and ROBERT LOPEZ

Half-time feel

The snow glows white on the moun-tain to-night, __ not a

foot-print __ to be seen. __ A king-dom of i - so-la -

- tion, and it looks like I'm the queen. __

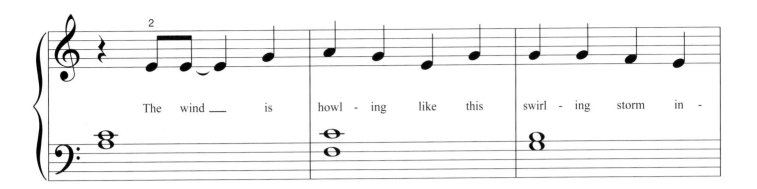

The wind __ is howl - ing like this swirl - ing storm in -

side. _____ Could - n't keep it in, _____ heav - en knows I ____

____ tried. Don't let ____ them

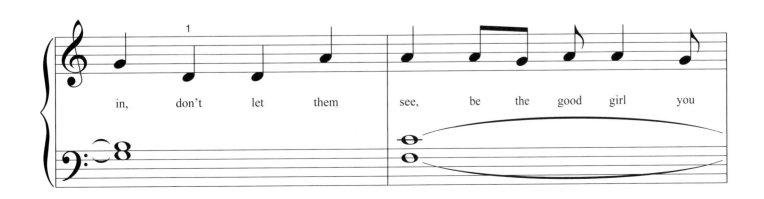

in, don't let them see, be the good girl you

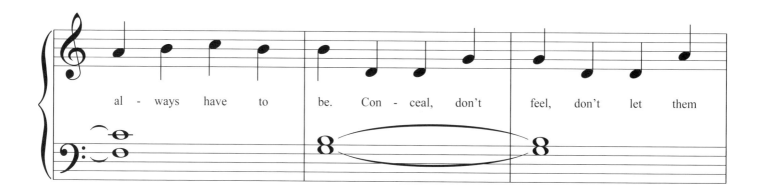

al - ways have to be. Con - ceal, don't feel, don't let them

know... Well, now they know.

Let it go, let it go, can't

hold it back an - y - more. Let it go, let it go,

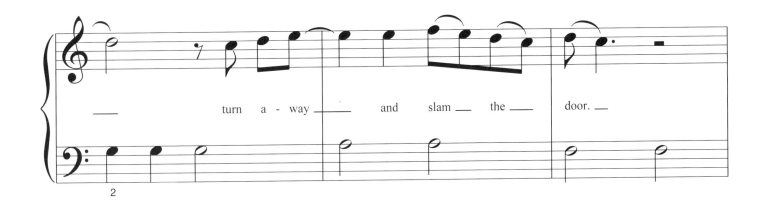

turn a - way and slam the door.

I don't care what they're going to say,

let the storm rage on. The

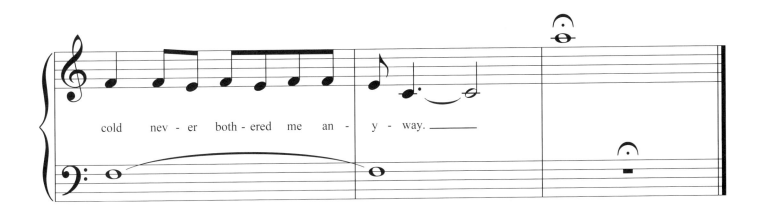

cold nev - er both - ered me an - y - way.

THAT'S HOW YOU KNOW

from ENCHANTED

Music by ALAN MENKEN
Lyrics by STEPHEN SCHWARTZ

Moderate Calypso

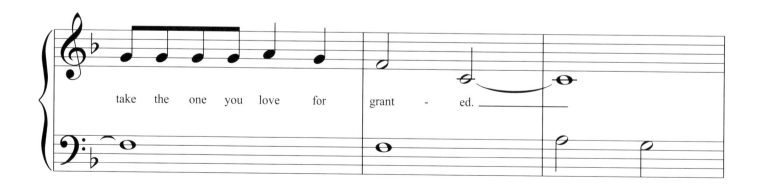

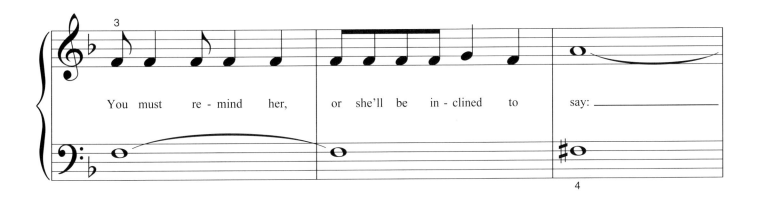

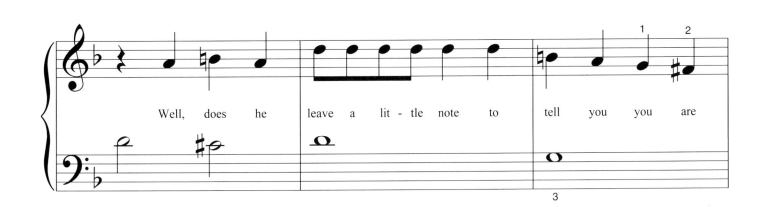

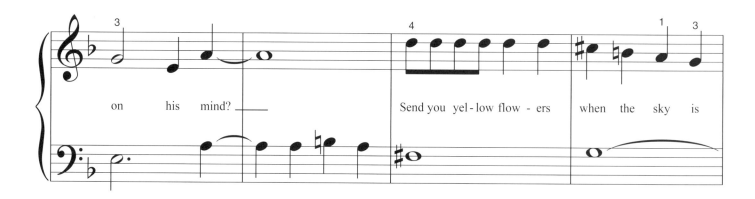

on his mind? ____ Send you yel-low flow - ers when the sky is

gray? Hey. ____ He'll find a new way to show you a

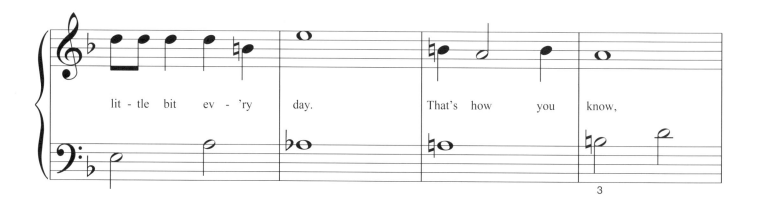

lit - tle bit ev - 'ry day. That's how you know,

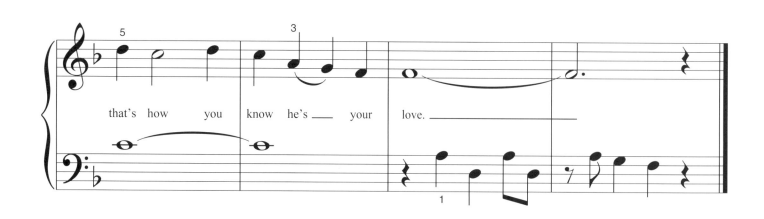

that's how you know he's ___ your love. ____

TOUCH THE SKY
from BRAVE

Music by ALEXANDER L. MANDEL
Lyrics by ALEXANDER L. MANDEL
and MARK ANDREWS

Moderately

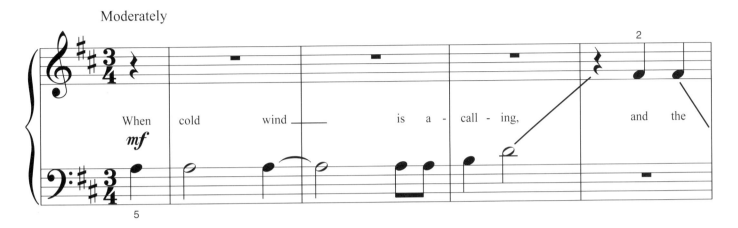

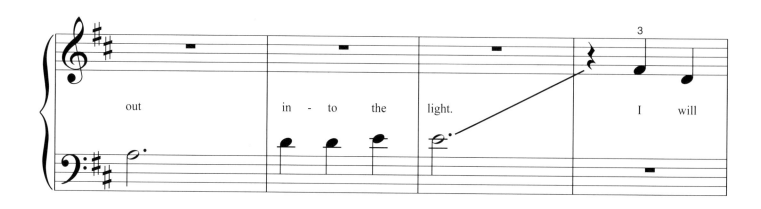

sky.   Na   na   na   na,   na   na

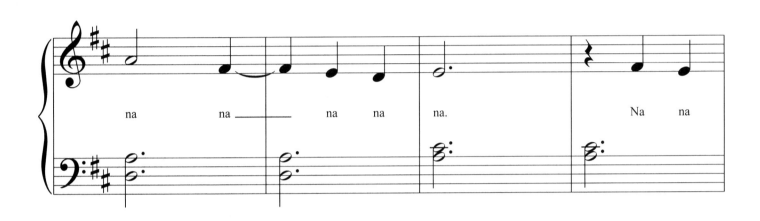

na   na _____ na   na   na.   Na   na

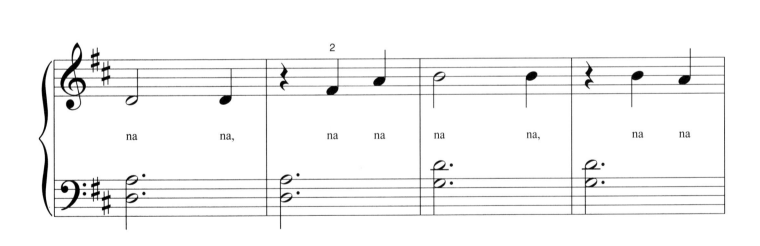

na   na,   na   na   na   na,   na   na

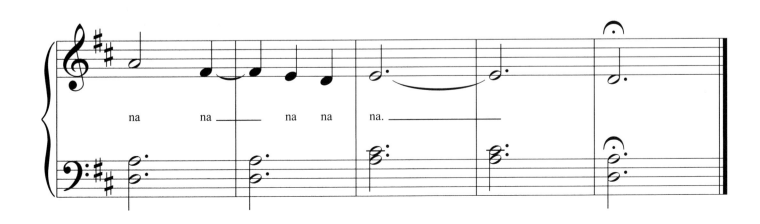

na   na _____ na   na   na. _____

WE BELONG TOGETHER

from TOY STORY 3 - A Pixar Film

Words and Music by
RANDY NEWMAN

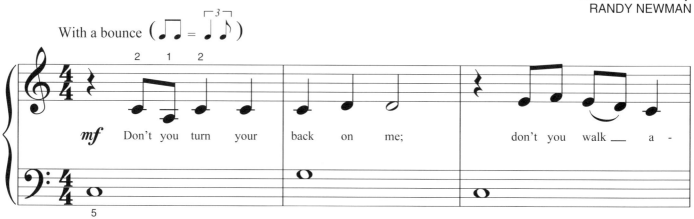

Just tell me you love me like I love you. You

know you do. _____ When we're to - geth - er, gray skies

clear up, and I cheer up to where I'm less de - pressed. _

And sin - cere - ly, from the bot - tom of my

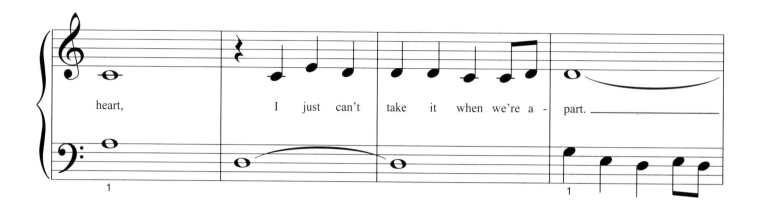

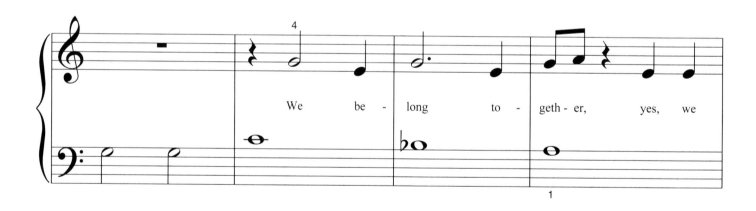

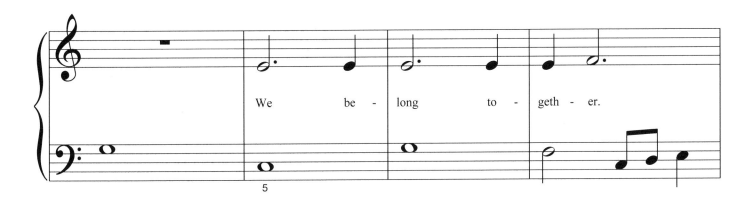

We be - long to - geth - er.

We be - long to -

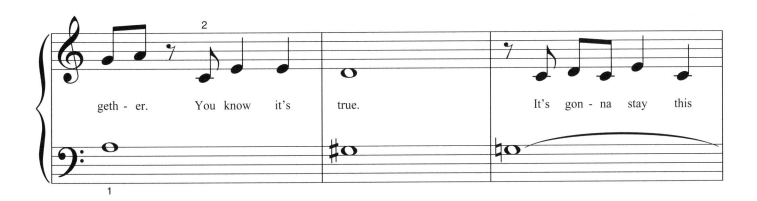

geth - er. You know it's true. It's gon - na stay this

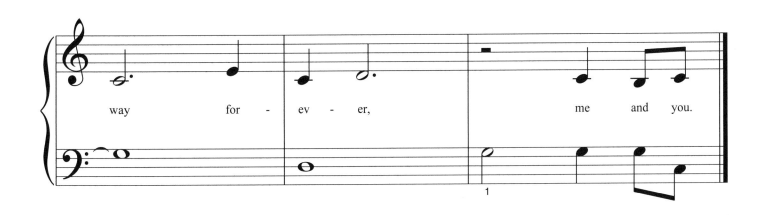

way for - ev - er, me and you.

WHEN WILL MY LIFE BEGIN?

from TANGLED

Music by ALAN MENKEN
Lyrics by GLENN SLATER

Moderately fast

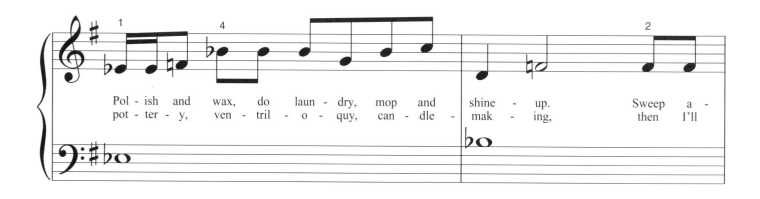

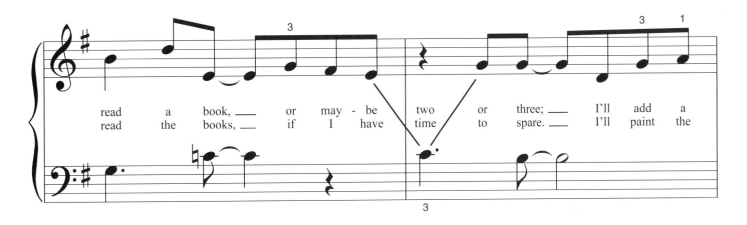

read   a   book, ___   or   may - be   two   or   three; ___   I'll   add   a
read   the   books, ___   if   I   have   time   to   spare. ___   I'll   paint   the

few   more   paint - ings   to   my   gal - ler - y; ___   I'll   play   gui -
walls   some   more; ___   I'm   sure   there's   room   some - where. ___   And   then   I'll

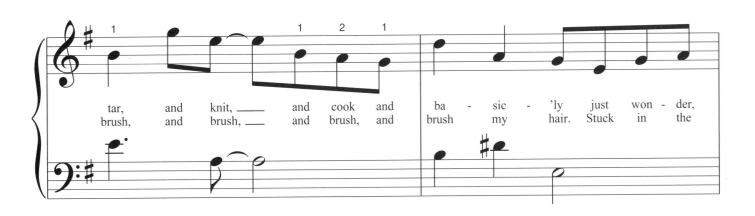

tar,   and   knit, ___   and   cook   and   ba - sic - 'ly   just   won - der,
brush,   and   brush, ___   and   brush, and   brush   my   hair. Stuck   in   the

"When   will   my   life   be - gin?"   To - mor - row
same   place   I've   al - ways   been.

night   the   lights   will   ap - pear,   just   like   they

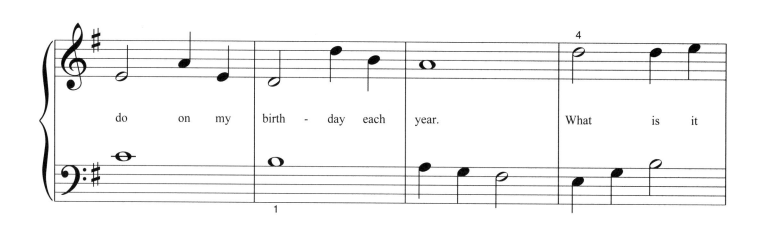

do   on   my   birth - day   each   year.   What   is   it

like   out   there   where   they   glow?   Now   that   I'm

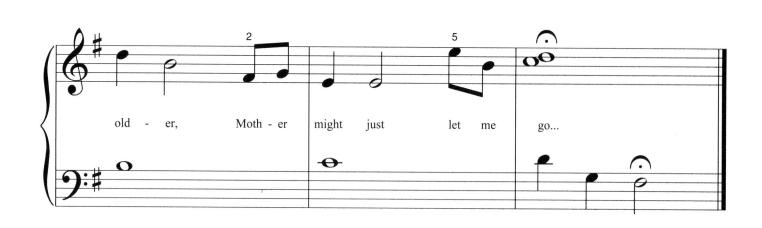

old - er,   Moth - er   might   just   let   me   go...